1 Barbie Dollhouse Plan Furniture

DENNIS L. DAY

TESTIMONIALS

Our dollhouse is terrific. Your plans are super!   Melodie Sherer

Your dollhouse beats any dollhouse on the market because it's so well built; it will be passed on for generations. We really like the rolling frame because Rachel can pull it out from the wall and put it back herself.   Susan Levy

Our girls 4 and 2 ½ love playing with their dollhouse everyday.   Melanie Hintz

She really enjoyed the house she got for Christmas, but then what 5 year old girl won't like a house taller than her. Thanks again for the great plans.   Chuck

It turned out so cute and was so much fun to make.   Terry Rife

My girls all love the finished product (and so do my wife and I). I appreciate the way your cutting layouts made use of the smallest amount of wood possible.   Mike Sparreo

What a fun project. I've given it to my granddaughter for her 4th birthday. She and her friends were all over it . . . very gratifying.   Art Wurfel

I wanted to send you a picture of the house. They really love it! Thanks a lot! Shannon Burke

Giving this dollhouse to my daughter made for a very exciting Christmas! Although she believes Santa's elves made it. In fact, all of the neighbors are quite impressed as well! Kay Ferguson

It has always been my dream to build a dollhouse for our little girls for Christmas. We had a great time building and painting and creating. We gave it to two girls who we knew needed a WOW for Christmas. I just wanted to write and let you know that we really enjoyed creating a great dollhouse keepsake. Thanks so much.   Rolfe and Janet Rankin

I have had my dollhouse for about two years. I like to decorate for different occasions with Christmas trees, pumpkins, rabbits, and other things. I have spent hours moving furniture and things around. My dollhouse is as good today as it was when I got it.   Sandra Tuman

Two years ago I purchased the large style dollhouse for my two daughters to share. This is a dollhouse which someday their own children will play with.   Sue Rogers

You've made many children happy. Our daughter has enjoyed her dollhouse . . . along with the many friends and cousins who have played with her. The house is superior to any other model dollhouse on the market. It is something that she will undoubtedly keep for her children.
                                    Carol and Kirk Witherspoon

The dollhouse you made for me is much better than the ones you get at the store. There are also steps which other dollhouses don't usually have.   Gwendolyn Witherspoon

I have had my dollhouse for about two years and have really enjoyed it. It is very sturdy and well constructed.   I am 45 years old and this dollhouse fulfilled a dream.   Sandra Tuman

Frequently Asked Questions

Q: Can I make a dollhouse and furniture if I haven't built anything before?

A: Yes, this has always been the objective. Someone with no background in woodworking is able to make a dollhouse with furniture that is functional for play, attractive, and will last from one generation to another. Dennis Day's plans make this possible. You can do it! Enjoy!

Q: How long does it take to make a dollhouse with furniture?

A: Allow one weekend to obtain materials, cut out materials, assemble dollhouse, and prime dollhouse. Allow a second weekend to paint and decorate. One person can complete a two story dollhouse from start to finish in thirty hours, and a three story dollhouse in forty hours. Furniture takes a day to make. If you have helpers you will finish quicker.

Q: Where do I obtain the items I need to build a dollhouse and furniture?

A: A local home center will have what you need. The items needed to build these dollhouses and furniture are readily available. Relax, you can do this. Reassurance is a good thing.

Q: Where do I get carpet for the rooms?

A: Local home centers or carpet stores carry carpet samples which they sell very reasonably. You can also use fabric, felt, or tile instead of carpet. Or paint the floors different colors. I liked two carpets for each room which allowed my daughters to empty the dollhouse and choose their carpet colors for the day for each room. Girls do love to decorate!

Q: Where do I find wallpaper?

A: Local home centers, wallpaper, and carpet stores have closeout single rolls of very expensive wallpaper for just a few dollars. Choose wallpaper with two dominant colors, and a small design. If your wallpaper has green and red in it, and you put a red carpet in the room then the red jumps out. If a green carpet is used then the green in the wallpaper jumps out. Great effect! Take your carpet samples with you to ensure a really good match with your wallpaper.

Q: Do I need special paint?

A: No, just buy regular latex semi-gloss paint. Let your dreams choose your colors.

Q: How do I know what materials to buy?

A: A helpful and detailed materials list is included in each plan, and is ideal to take to your local home center when purchasing materials.

Q: Do I need fancy or expensive tools?

A: No, inexpensive power hand tools will do the job. The hand tools needed are a jig saw, drill, sander, and a hammer.

Enjoy!

Dennis Day

Dennis L. Day

Drawings, instructions, and pictures Corel Corporation.

DESCRIPTION
Barbie™ Dollhouse Plan Furniture

Use this 1 plan to create sturdy and beautiful Wooden Barbie™ Dollhouse Furniture that dreams are made of with this Easy To Build plan. This Do-It-Yourself plan has step-by-step easy to follow instructions. The accompanying drawings and pictures make for easy assembly by the experienced and inexperienced individual. This durable and lovely dollhouse furniture is made of 3/4", ½", and 3/8" plywood. A helpful and detailed materials list is included and is ideal to take to your local home center when purchasing materials. You can build this Wooden Barbie™ Dollhouse Furniture using the simple easy to use hand tools of a jig saw, sander, drill, and hammer. The finished Dollhouse Furniture will reflect your individual decorating taste. This Dollhouse Furniture is designed to be used with the 11 ½" Barbie™ Dolls, the 11 ½" High School Musical™ Dolls, and other 11 ½" fashion dolls. Any toy that is Playscale™ 2" = 1' (1/6 scale) in height can be used with this Wooden Barbie™ Dollhouse Furniture. This dollhouse furniture will provide years of enjoyment and be passed on for generations . . . Your Child's Window to the World!

About the Author

Dennis L. Day is the author of several Easy To Build plan books for making Wooden Barbie™ Dollhouses, Wooden Barbie™ Dollhouse Furniture, Wooden Barbie™ Castles, Wooden Action Figure Castles, and Wooden Barns. These Do-It-Yourself plans have step-by-step easy to follow instructions with accompanying drawings and pictures for easy assembly by the experienced and inexperienced individual. His plans are designed for use with the 11 ½" Barbie™ Dolls, the 11 ½" High School Musical™ Dolls, and other 11 ½" fashion dolls. A toy that is 1/6 scale (called Playscale™ 2" = 1') or a toy less than 15" in height (i.e. 10" Bratz™ Dolls) can be used with these Wooden Barbie™ Dollhouses. His Wooden Barbie™ Castles and Wooden Action Figure Castles can be used with a toy less than 16" in height. He made his first Wooden Barbie™ Dollhouse with ½" plywood for his oldest daughter in 1987. His youngest daughter wanted a log home style Wooden Barbie™ Dollhouse which she helped design. His daughters had a furniture problem. They would place Barbie™ on her plastic furniture and Barbie™ would fall over. Not much fun. To solve this problem he made wooden kitchen and living room furniture that kept Barbie™ upright. His girls encouraged him to make more furniture. He did. His two oldest sons helped with the planning and the playing of their own castles. The fifth and final child was a son, and he found many good times were waiting for him. Wonderful memories!
    Dennis L. Day has a B.S. and M.A. from the University of Iowa. His five children are grown, and the first Grandchild was born March 14, 2008, a boy. He currently lives in St. Cloud, MN.

D E D I C A T I O N

To our children and our grandchildren and to everyone who makes the effort everyday.
Dennis Day

The ambitions of people who never became very rich, who founded no dynasty or long-lasting company, and who lived in the middle and lower ranks of the business world, are difficult to write about, because they are seldom recorded. But the character of a society is greatly influenced by the form the ambitions of such men take, and by the extent to which they are satisfied or frustrated. THEODORE ZELDEN : 1848-1945 : Ambition and Love

HARDCOPY
BOOKS
by
Dennis L. Day
available at
www.lulu.com/dollhouse

download
books
by
Dennis L. Day
at
www.lulu.com/dollhouse

denday57@hotmail.com

A M O S T   I M P O R T A N T   R E Q U E S T

Twenty-one years ago my oldest daughter was insistent and persistent that she needed a dollhouse for her Barbie™. We looked locally and found plastic. Not good. I made my first Wooden Barbie™ Dollhouse because my adorable daughter was insistent and persistent, and I loved her. She played with her Barbie™ Dollhouse more than I thought humanly possible. I started making Barbie™ Dollhouses, Furniture, Castles, and a Barn for my children and later for other children, and adults. It is one of the best things I ever did, and still meaningful.

A customer suggested that I share customer pictures and insights. Great idea! The best for me is a photo of a beaming child next to a dollhouse made just for her using my plan. Very gratifying. Sharing photos is enjoyable for everyone. And personal insights reassure others that my Barbie™ Dollhouses are worthwhile and quite doable. Please take time to send me your photos and personal insights. I look forward to hearing from you. Thanks so much for sharing your Barbie™ Dollhouse and the joy created.

Sincerely yours,

Dennis Day

Dennis Day

CONTENTS

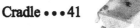

1 Barbie™ Dollhouse Plan Furniture

8

FURNITURE PLANS

My daughters had a furniture problem. They would place Barbie™ on her plastic furniture and she would fall over. Not much fun. To solve this problem I made kitchen and living room wooden furniture that kept Barbie™ upright. My girls encouraged me to make more. Enjoy!

- **LIVING ROOM** 11-14
  - regular chair, couch, and rocking chair
    - fits:
      - 3 Story Dollhouse
      - 2 Story Dollhouse

- **KITCHEN** 15-24
  - kitchen table and chairs
    - fits:
      - 3 Story Dollhouse
      - 2 Story Dollhouse

- **ALL ROOMS** 25-26
  - fireplace
    - fits:
      - 3 Story Dollhouse
      - 2 Story Dollhouse

- **BEDROOM** 28-42
  - single regular bed and cradle
    - fits:
      - 3 Story Dollhouse
      - 2 Story Dollhouse

  - single and double canopy bed, and double regular bed
    - fits:
      - 3 Story Dollhouse

FURNITURE
The first objective is to purchase the materials needed to build your Furniture.
ITEMS YOU WILL NEED TO OBTAIN

SAFETY FIRST
THE SAFE WAY IS
THE BEST WAY

Quantity	Description

TOOLS
1 each	Dust mask, hearing protector, and safety glasses or face shield.
1	Jigsaw with bits for wood smooth finish.
1	Drill with bits 1/4", and 1/16" (extra 1/16" bits good idea as it breaks easy).
1	Electric Sander and 3 packages of 60 grid sandpaper.
1 each	Hammer and nail punch to sink brad heads (nails) below surface.
1 each	Tape measure, ruler 12" and a 4' straight edge.
6	Wooden pencils and one pencil sharpener.
1	Wide tip sharpie black permanent marker for outlining fireplace bricks.
1	Putty knife to apply Durham's Water Putty.
1	Table to assemble furniture upon.

PRIMER, PAINT, and PAINT ACCESSORIES
Note: You will need at least one paint stir stick for primer and each paint color.

1	Quart of latex primer (sealer).
1	Pint of stain color of your choice for each piece of furniture.

• • • Note: No primer (sealer) needed when using stain. • • •

1	Pint of latex semi-gloss paint color of your choice for each piece of furniture.
1 each	Paint brushes 1/4", ½", and 1" for applying paint and/or stain to furniture.

• • • Note: One coat of primer is enough. Primer is very thin when applied. It is not paint so do not be alarmed if after one coat you can see through it as this is normal. Primer is a sealer not a paint. Putting on too thick a coat of primer or paint, or not allowing either to dry between coats could result in paint peeling off. Apply one thin coat of primer followed by thin coats of paint works great. One thick coat is quicker to apply but won't adhere properly. • • •

ADHESIVE, GLUE, and PUTTY
1	Large bottle of yellow wood glue to assemble furniture.
1	Small can of Durham's Water Putty to cover #17 brad heads and wood joints.
1	Tube of Power Grab Construction Adhesive by Loctite to assemble furniture if not using yellow wood glue.

WOOD
1 bag	Old fashion one piece wooden clothespins (page 173).
1 each	Plywood boards: 3/4" x 12" x 12", 3/8" x 24" x 48", 1/4" x 12" x 48"
1	2 x 2 - 36" (actual dimensions 1 5/8" x 1 1/4" x 36") (makes 7 fireplaces)
1	1 x 3 - 48" (actual dimensions 3/4" x 2 ½" x 36") (makes 7 fireplaces)
1 each	1 1/4" dowel x 9" for kitchen chairs and 3/4" dowel x 18" for kitchen table
1 each	1/4" dowel x 48" (one for each canopy bed: 2 beds = 2 dowels, 4 beds = 4 dowels)

WIRE BRADS (NAILS)
1 box	Wire brads for assembling furniture # 17 - 1"

MISCELLANEOUS
1 each	2/3 yard fabric and ½" batting for all furniture (match or contrast curtains).
1 each	Package needles, thread to match each fabric, and scissors.
1	Roll of paper towel.

10

FURNITURE: COUCH & CHAIR

SCAN, COPY, or REMOVE THIS PAGE.
THEN CUT OUT PATTERN.

TWO 1/4" DOWELS
BOTH 4 3/4" FOR CHAIR
OR
TWO 1/4" DOWELS
BOTH 10 1/4" FOR COUCH

DOWEL GOES
THROUGH
SIDE PIECES

MAIN SUPPORT
BUTTS AGAINST
SIDE PIECES

BRADS

MAIN SUPPORT

Note: Once assembled
use Durham's Water Putty
over dowel ends and #17
brad heads on sides.

3/8"

4" (chair)   4 3/4" (chair)
9 ½" (couch)   10 1/4" (couch)

3/8"

4" (chair)

9 ½" (couch)

3/4"

1 3/4"

9 1/2"

4"

COUCH
MAIN
SUPPORT
IS 9 ½"

M
A
I
N

S
U
P
P
O
R
T

CHAIR
MAIN
SUPPORT
IS 4"

1/4" HOLE

PATTERN

3/4"

Drill 1/16" pilot holes

1/4" HOLE

3/8" WOOD
COUCH, CHAIR,
and ROCKER

BRADS

1 3/4"

USE DOTTED LINES
FOR ROCKER

Note: Finished
couch is 10 1/4"
wide. Finished
chair and rocker
are 4 3/4" wide.
All are
assembled
the same.

11

FURNITURE

SCAN or COPY PAGE 11,
or
REMOVE THIS PAGE
TO OBTAIN
COUCH, CHAIR, and ROCKER PATTERN
ON PAGE 11.

THEN CUT OUT
COUCH, CHAIR, and ROCKER PATTERN
ON PAGE 11.

FURNITURE: COUCH & CHAIR

CHAIR and COUCH SUPPORT

1. Sew 1" seams on A's.
2. Fold ½" under on B side then fold back on B line and sew along ½" fold forming casing.

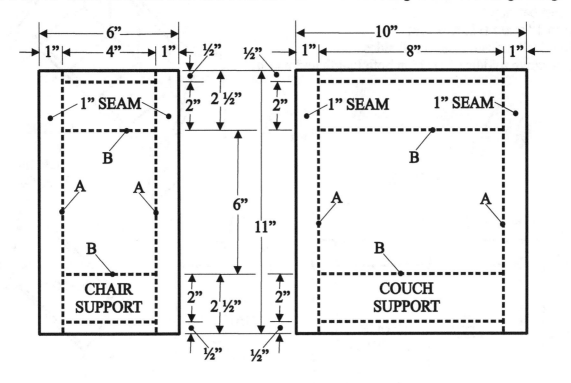

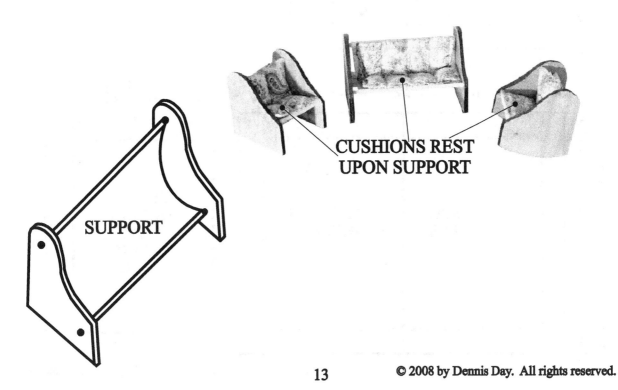

CUSHIONS REST
UPON SUPPORT

SUPPORT

13

FURNITURE: COUCH & CHAIR

CHAIR and COUCH CUSHION

1. Fold on fold line wrong side shows.
2. Sew A and C.
3. Turn inside out so right side shows.
4. Insert batting.
5. Turn 1" seam B in and sew.
6. Sew 1/4" in from edge on all sides.
7. Sew down middle of cushion both length and width.

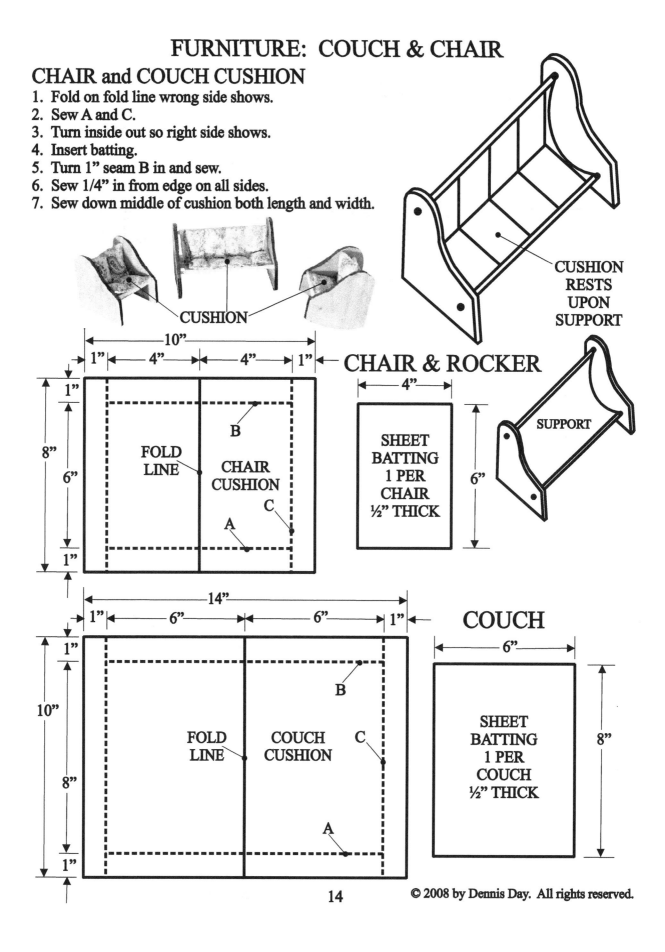

CUSHION

CUSHION RESTS UPON SUPPORT

CHAIR & ROCKER

10"
1" 4" 4" 1"
1"
8"
6"
FOLD LINE
B
CHAIR CUSHION
C
A
1"

4"
SHEET BATTING 1 PER CHAIR ½" THICK
6"

SUPPORT

COUCH

14"
1" 6" 6" 1"
1"
10"
FOLD LINE
B
COUCH CUSHION
C
A
8"
1"

6"
SHEET BATTING 1 PER COUCH ½" THICK
8"

14

FURNITURE: KITCHEN TABLE

5 3/8"

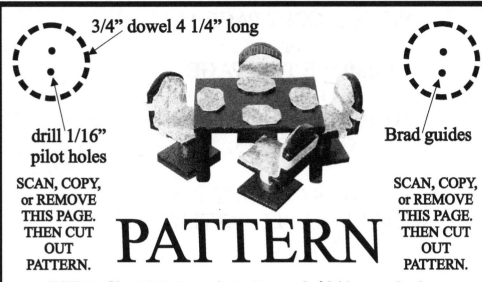

3/4" dowel 4 1/4" long

drill 1/16"
pilot holes

Brad guides

PATTERN

8 1/8"

KITCHEN TABLE 3/8" WOOD

1. Cut out table top 3/8" wood using this PATTERN.
2. Cut 3/4" dowel 4 1/4" long. Quantity needed is
   four for table legs.
3. Glue, drill pilot holes, and nail dowels to table.
   Use # 17 brads 1" long. Note: Dowel is 3/16" from
   edges. Use brad guides on this PATTERN to locate
   brad placement on table top.
4. Sink #17 brad heads below surface with nail punch
   then putty over with Durham's Water Putty. Let dry.
   Sand and stain, or sand, prime and paint.

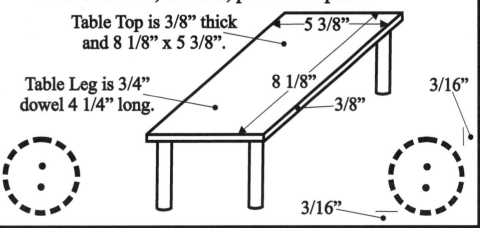

Table Top is 3/8" thick
and 8 1/8" x 5 3/8".

5 3/8"

Table Leg is 3/4"
dowel 4 1/4" long.

8 1/8"

3/8"

3/16"

3/16"

FURNITURE

SCAN or COPY PAGE 15,
or
REMOVE THIS PAGE
TO OBTAIN
KITCHEN TABLE PATTERN
ON PAGE 15.

THEN CUT OUT
KITCHEN TABLE PATTERN
ON PAGE 15.

16

FURNITURE: KITCHEN TABLE PLACE MATS - NEED 4

1. Cut out eight pieces.
2. Place two pieces right sides together.
3. Sew a 1/4" seam, A to B, leaving a 1" space.
4. Turn place mat inside out, turn in rest of 1/4" seam.
5. Top stitch 1/8" from edge all around place mat.

SCAN, COPY, or REMOVE THIS PAGE. THEN CUT OUT PATTERN.

PATTERN

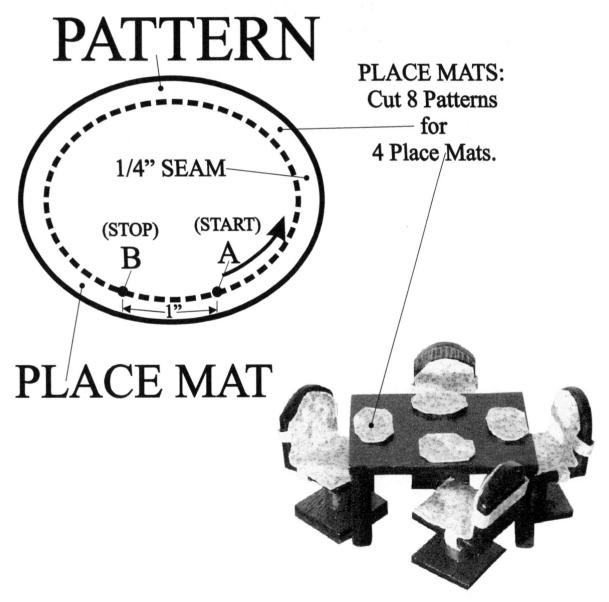

PLACE MATS:
Cut 8 Patterns
for
4 Place Mats.

1/4" SEAM

(STOP)
B

(START)
A

1"

PLACE MAT

FURNITURE

SCAN or COPY PAGE 17,
or
REMOVE THIS PAGE
TO OBTAIN
PLACE MAT PATTERN
ON PAGE 17.

THEN CUT OUT
PLACE MAT PATTERN
ON PAGE 17.

FURNITURE: KITCHEN CHAIR

1. Cut out BASE 3/4" wood using PATTERN C. 2. Cut out BACK 3/8" wood using PATTERN A.
3. Cut out SEAT 3/8" wood using PATTERN B. 4. Cut 1 1/4" dowel rod 2" long.
5. Glue then nail BACK to SEAT using dotted lines for placement PATTERN B. Drill pilot holes then use two # 17 brads 1" and nail. 6. Sink brad heads below surface with nail punch and cover with Durham's Water Putty. Let dry. Sand and stain, or sand, prime, and paint.

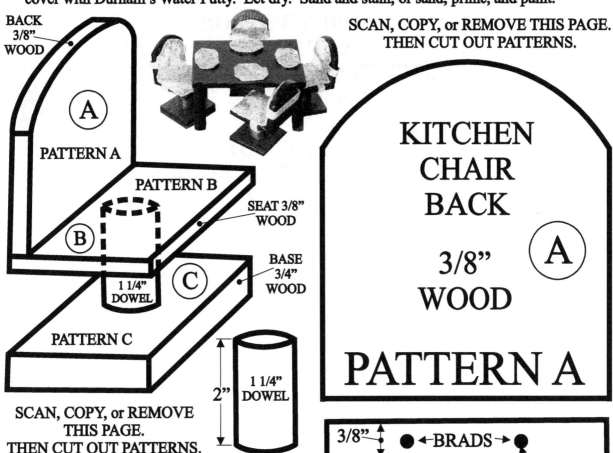

SCAN, COPY, or REMOVE THIS PAGE.
THEN CUT OUT PATTERNS.

KITCHEN CHAIR BACK

3/8" WOOD

Ⓐ

PATTERN A

SCAN, COPY, or REMOVE THIS PAGE.
THEN CUT OUT PATTERNS.

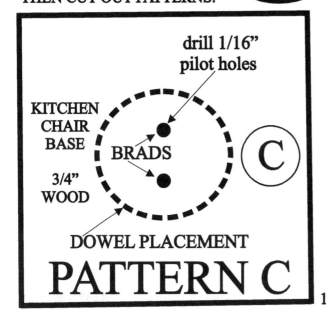

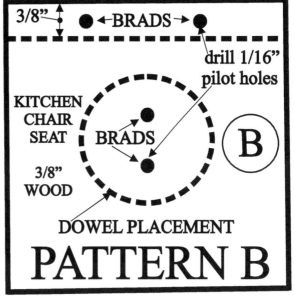

FURNITURE

SCAN or COPY PAGE 19,
or
REMOVE THIS PAGE
TO OBTAIN
KITCHEN CHAIR PATTERNS
ON PAGE 19.

THEN CUT OUT
KITCHEN CHAIR PATTERNS
ON PAGE 19.

FURNITURE: KITCHEN CHAIR CUSHION

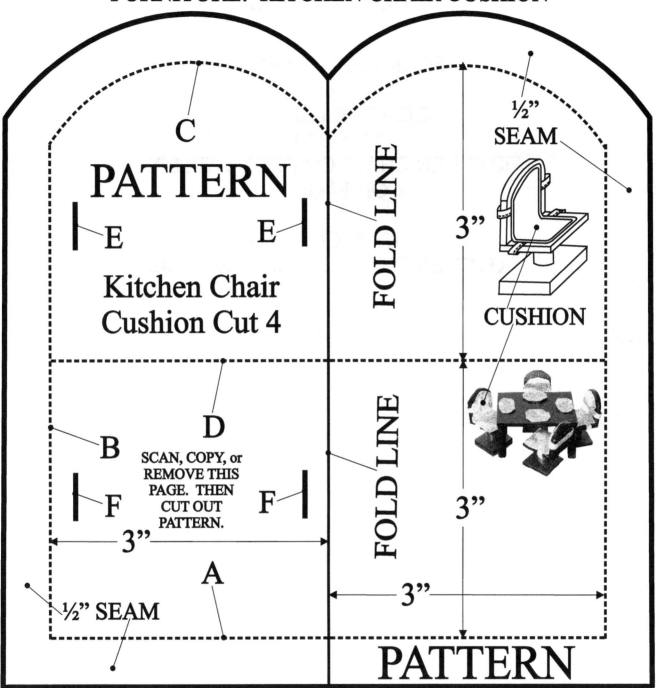

C

PATTERN

E   E

Kitchen Chair
Cushion Cut 4

FOLD LINE

½"
SEAM

3"

CUSHION

B

D

SCAN, COPY, or
REMOVE THIS
PAGE. THEN
CUT OUT
PATTERN.

F   F

FOLD LINE

3"

3"

A

½" SEAM

3"

PATTERN

1. Fold on fold line with right side together.
2. Sew ½" seam on B, C.
3. Turn.
4. Fold ½" seam in on A and top stitch cushion 1/4" from edge.
   Top stitch the rest of the other edges. Top stitch along D line.

FURNITURE

SCAN or COPY PAGE 21,
or
REMOVE THIS PAGE
TO OBTAIN
KITCHEN CHAIR CUSHION PATTERN
ON PAGE 21.

THEN CUT OUT
KITCHEN CHAIR CUSHION PATTERN
ON PAGE 21.

FURNITURE: KITCHEN CHAIR CUSHION LOOPS

1. Fold on fold line with right sides on outside turn ½" seam in and top stitch 1/8".
2. On backside of cushion sew loops on E and F (page 21).

SCAN, COPY, or REMOVE THIS PAGE. THEN CUT OUT PATTERN.

½" SEAM	LOOP PATTERN
FOLD LINE	
½" SEAM	CUT 2 PER CHAIR

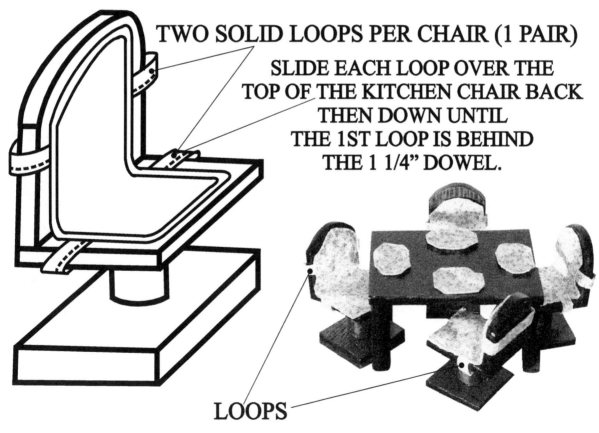

TWO SOLID LOOPS PER CHAIR (1 PAIR)

SLIDE EACH LOOP OVER THE
TOP OF THE KITCHEN CHAIR BACK
THEN DOWN UNTIL
THE 1ST LOOP IS BEHIND
THE 1 1/4" DOWEL.

LOOPS

FURNITURE

SCAN or COPY PAGE 23,
or
REMOVE THIS PAGE
TO OBTAIN
KITCHEN CHAIR CUSHION LOOP PATTERN
ON PAGE 23.

THEN CUT OUT
KITCHEN CHAIR CUSHION LOOP PATTERN
ON PAGE 23.

24

FURNITURE: FIREPLACE - WORKS IN EVERY ROOM

Cut wood materials to length for the Fireplace.

Quantity	Description
2	2" x 2" - 4" long for both S (actual 1 5/8" by 1 ½" x 4" long)
1	2" x 2" - 2 ½" long for HT (actual 1 5/8" by 1 ½" x 2 ½" long)
1	1" x 3" - 6 5/8" long for M (actual 3/4" by 2 ½" x 6 5/8" long)
1	5 3/4" x 4" x 1/4" thick for B
1	2 ½" x 1 ½" x 1/4" thick for HB
10	Brads # 17 - 1" long

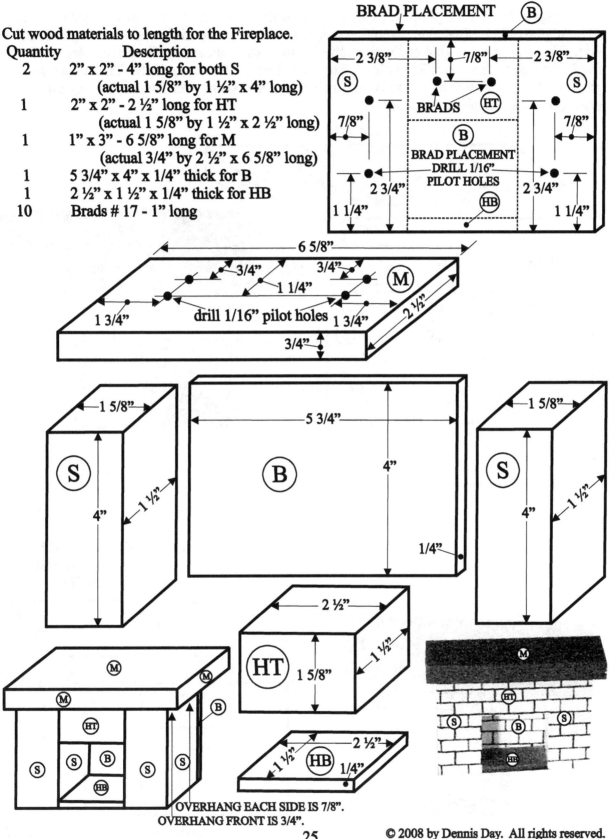

OVERHANG EACH SIDE IS 7/8".
OVERHANG FRONT IS 3/4".

25

FURNITURE: FIREPLACE - WORKS IN EVERY ROOM

Using pages 25-26 drill pilot holes with 1/16" drill bit in M & B then assemble fireplace without glue or brads (nails) to determine proper fit. Once proper fit is achieved set pieces off to side. Next apply wood glue or Loctite adhesive to B and reassemble Fireplace. Nail # 17 - 1" Brads through back side of B to hold all fireplace pieces S, S, HT, and HB. Then attach M with glue and Brads. Countersink Brads with nail punch and putty over Brads. Let dry then sand, prime, paint, and apply brick pattern.

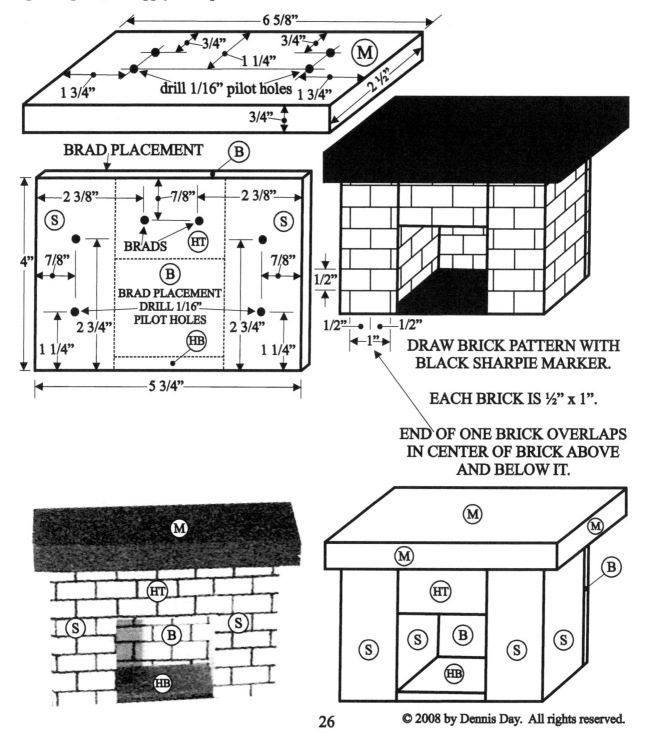

DRAW BRICK PATTERN WITH BLACK SHARPIE MARKER.

EACH BRICK IS ½" x 1".

END OF ONE BRICK OVERLAPS IN CENTER OF BRICK ABOVE AND BELOW IT.

FURNITURE

SCAN or COPY PAGE 28,
or
REMOVE THIS PAGE
TO OBTAIN
SINGLE BED HEADBOARD and FOOTBOARD PATTERNS
ON PAGE 28.

THEN CUT OUT
SINGLE BED HEADBOARD and FOOTBOARD PATTERNS
ON PAGE 28.

FURNITURE: PATTERN SINGLE BED HEADBOARD & FOOTBOARD

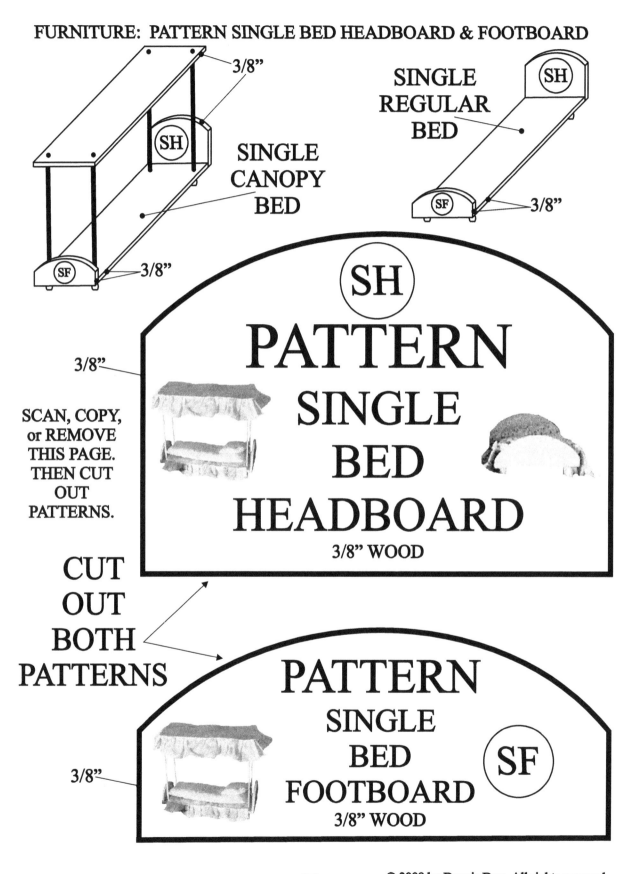

SINGLE
CANOPY
BED

3/8"

3/8"

SF

3/8"

SINGLE
REGULAR
BED

SH

SF

3/8"

3/8"

SCAN, COPY,
or REMOVE
THIS PAGE.
THEN CUT
OUT
PATTERNS.

CUT
OUT
BOTH
PATTERNS

SH

PATTERN
SINGLE
BED
HEADBOARD
3/8" WOOD

PATTERN
SINGLE
BED
FOOTBOARD
3/8" WOOD

SF

3/8"

28

FURNITURE:
SINGLE BED MATTRESS SUPPORT - 3/8" WOOD
and/or
SINGLE BED CANOPY SUPPORT - 3/8" WOOD

3/8"

3/8"

SINGLE BED MATTRESS SUPPORT

(MS)

3/8"

1/4"

7/8"

NOTE:
OPTION ONE:
7/8" DOWEL
ROD INSERT
FOR
CLOTHESPIN
BED LEGS
(PAGE 34).

NOTE:
OPTION
TWO:
17 BRAD
1" FOR
CLOTHESPIN
BED LEGS
(PAGE 35).

13"

½"   ½"

1/16" PILOT HOLE
17 - 1" BRAD
OR
1/4" HOLE FOR
1/4" DOWEL ROD

½"   ½"

(MS) SINGLE BED
MATTRESS SUPPORT
3/8" WOOD

AND

(CS) SINGLE BED
CANOPY SUPPORT
3/8" WOOD

SINGLE BED CANOPY SUPPORT

3/8"   3/8"

(CS)

3/8"

(MS)

NOTE: USE
CLOTHESPIN WITH
DOWEL ROD
INSERT FOR
CLOTHESPIN
BED LEGS
(PAGE 33).

3/8"

½"

1/16" PILOT HOLE
17 - 1" BRAD
OR
1/4" HOLE FOR
1/4" DOWEL ROD

½"

½"   ½"

5"

NOTE: 11 1/4" DOWEL ROD INSERTS THROUGH MATTRESS
SUPPORT AND INTO CLOTHESPIN BED LEG.

1/4"

CANOPY DOWEL ROD   NEED 4

11 1/4"

29

FURNITURE:
DOUBLE BED MATTRESS SUPPORT
and/or
DOUBLE BED CANOPY SUPPORT

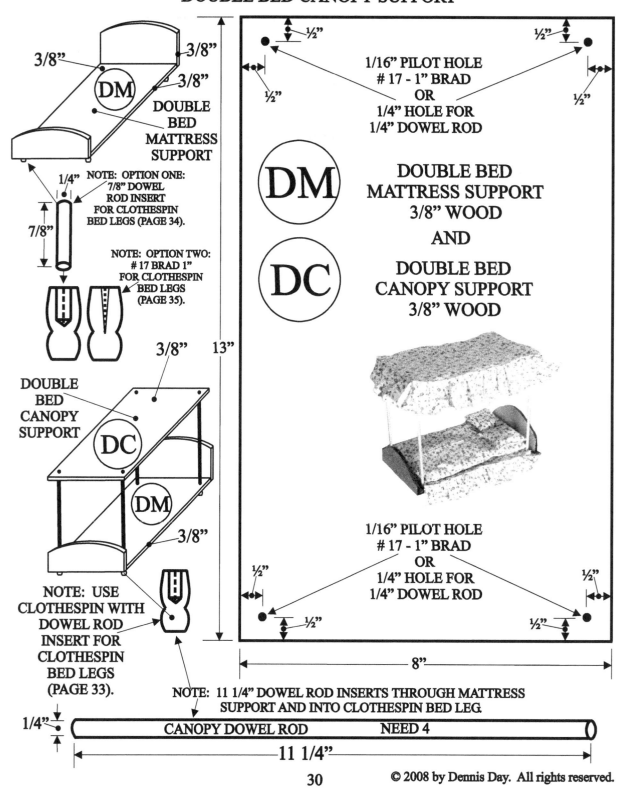

3/8"

3/8"

3/8"

DM

DOUBLE BED MATTRESS SUPPORT

1/4"

7/8"

NOTE: OPTION ONE: 7/8" DOWEL ROD INSERT FOR CLOTHESPIN BED LEGS (PAGE 34).

NOTE: OPTION TWO: # 17 BRAD 1" FOR CLOTHESPIN BED LEGS (PAGE 35).

3/8"

DOUBLE BED CANOPY SUPPORT

DC

DM

3/8"

NOTE: USE CLOTHESPIN WITH DOWEL ROD INSERT FOR CLOTHESPIN BED LEGS (PAGE 33).

½"   ½"

½"

1/16" PILOT HOLE
17 - 1" BRAD
OR
1/4" HOLE FOR
1/4" DOWEL ROD

½"   ½"

½"

DM

DC

DOUBLE BED MATTRESS SUPPORT 3/8" WOOD

AND

DOUBLE BED CANOPY SUPPORT 3/8" WOOD

13"

1/16" PILOT HOLE
17 - 1" BRAD
OR
1/4" HOLE FOR
1/4" DOWEL ROD

½"   ½"

½"   ½"

8"

NOTE: 11 1/4" DOWEL ROD INSERTS THROUGH MATTRESS SUPPORT AND INTO CLOTHESPIN BED LEG.

1/4"

CANOPY DOWEL ROD   NEED 4

11 1/4"

30

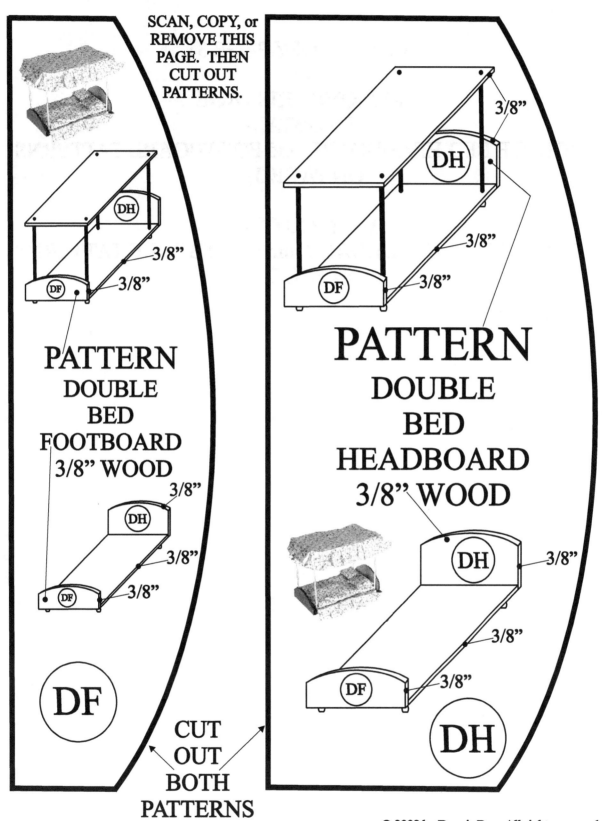

SCAN, COPY, or REMOVE THIS PAGE. THEN CUT OUT PATTERNS.

3/8"

DH

3/8"

3/8"

DF

3/8"

3/8"

PATTERN
DOUBLE
BED
FOOTBOARD
3/8" WOOD

3/8"

DH

3/8"

3/8"

DF

DF

PATTERN
DOUBLE
BED
HEADBOARD
3/8" WOOD

DH

3/8"

3/8"

DF

3/8"

DH

CUT OUT BOTH PATTERNS

31

FURNITURE

SCAN or COPY PAGE 31,
or
REMOVE THIS PAGE
TO OBTAIN
DOUBLE BED HEADBOARD and FOOTBOARD PATTERNS
ON PAGE 31.

THEN CUT OUT
DOUBLE BED HEADBOARD and FOOTBOARD PATTERNS
ON PAGE 31.

FURNITURE: CLOTHESPIN BED LEGS
FOR
SINGLE CANOPY BED AND DOUBLE CANOPY BED
USING
CANOPY DOWEL 1/4" x 11 1/4"

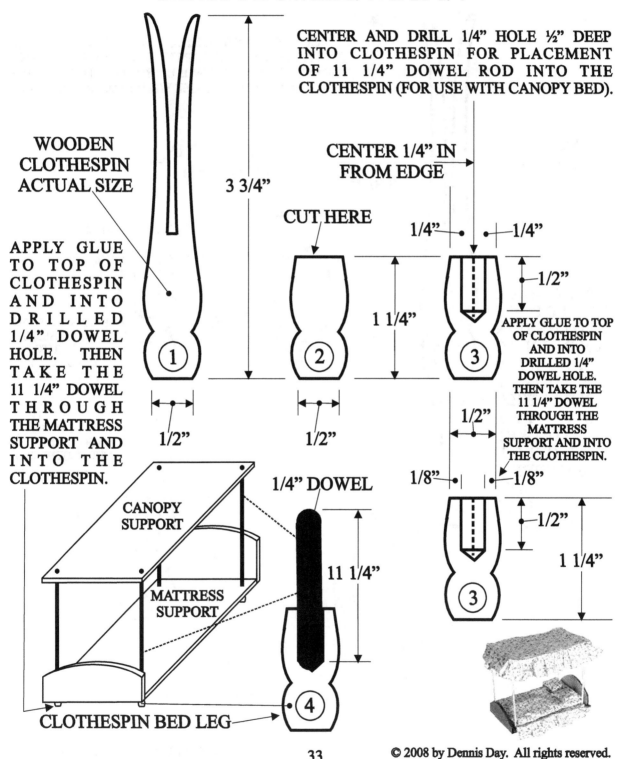

CENTER AND DRILL 1/4" HOLE ½" DEEP INTO CLOTHESPIN FOR PLACEMENT OF 11 1/4" DOWEL ROD INTO THE CLOTHESPIN (FOR USE WITH CANOPY BED).

WOODEN CLOTHESPIN ACTUAL SIZE

CENTER 1/4" IN FROM EDGE

3 3/4"

APPLY GLUE TO TOP OF CLOTHESPIN AND INTO DRILLED 1/4" DOWEL HOLE. THEN TAKE THE 11 1/4" DOWEL THROUGH THE MATTRESS SUPPORT AND INTO THE CLOTHESPIN.

CUT HERE

1/4"   1/4"

1/2"

1 1/4"

APPLY GLUE TO TOP OF CLOTHESPIN AND INTO DRILLED 1/4" DOWEL HOLE. THEN TAKE THE 11 1/4" DOWEL THROUGH THE MATTRESS SUPPORT AND INTO THE CLOTHESPIN.

1/2"

1/2"

1/2"

1/8"   1/8"

1/2"

1 1/4"

CANOPY SUPPORT

1/4" DOWEL

11 1/4"

MATTRESS SUPPORT

CLOTHESPIN BED LEG

33

FURNITURE: CLOTHESPIN BED LEGS
FOR
SINGLE REGULAR BED AND DOUBLE REGULAR BED (NO CANOPY)
USING
DOWEL 1/4" x 7/8"

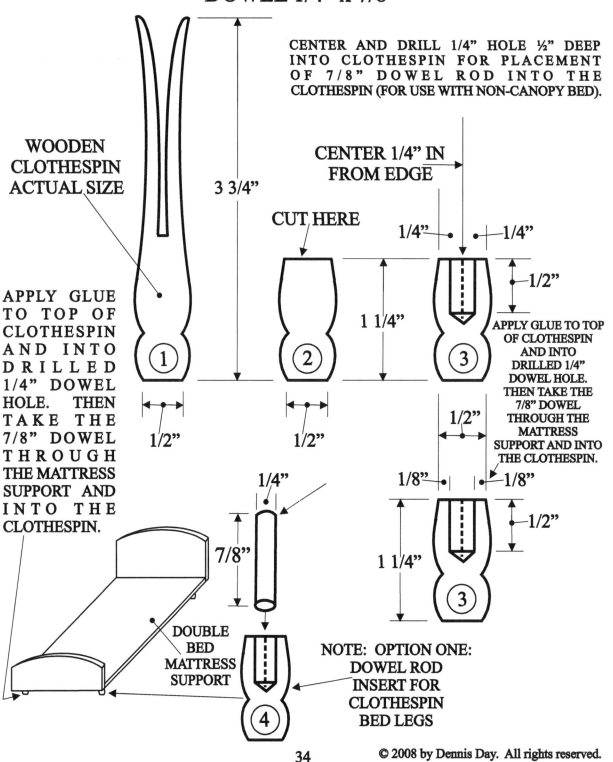

CENTER AND DRILL 1/4" HOLE ½" DEEP INTO CLOTHESPIN FOR PLACEMENT OF 7/8" DOWEL ROD INTO THE CLOTHESPIN (FOR USE WITH NON-CANOPY BED).

WOODEN CLOTHESPIN ACTUAL SIZE

3 3/4"

CENTER 1/4" IN FROM EDGE

CUT HERE

1/4"   1/4"

1/2"

1 1/4"

APPLY GLUE TO TOP OF CLOTHESPIN AND INTO DRILLED 1/4" DOWEL HOLE.   THEN TAKE THE 7/8" DOWEL THROUGH THE MATTRESS SUPPORT AND INTO THE CLOTHESPIN.

APPLY GLUE TO TOP OF CLOTHESPIN AND INTO DRILLED 1/4" DOWEL HOLE. THEN TAKE THE 7/8" DOWEL THROUGH THE MATTRESS SUPPORT AND INTO THE CLOTHESPIN.

1/2"

1/2"

1/2"

1/4"

7/8"

1/8"   1/8"

1/2"

1 1/4"

DOUBLE BED MATTRESS SUPPORT

NOTE: OPTION ONE: DOWEL ROD INSERT FOR CLOTHESPIN BED LEGS

34

FURNITURE: CLOTHESPIN BED LEGS
FOR
SINGLE REGULAR BED AND DOUBLE REGULAR BED (NO CANOPY)
USING
17 - 1" BRADS

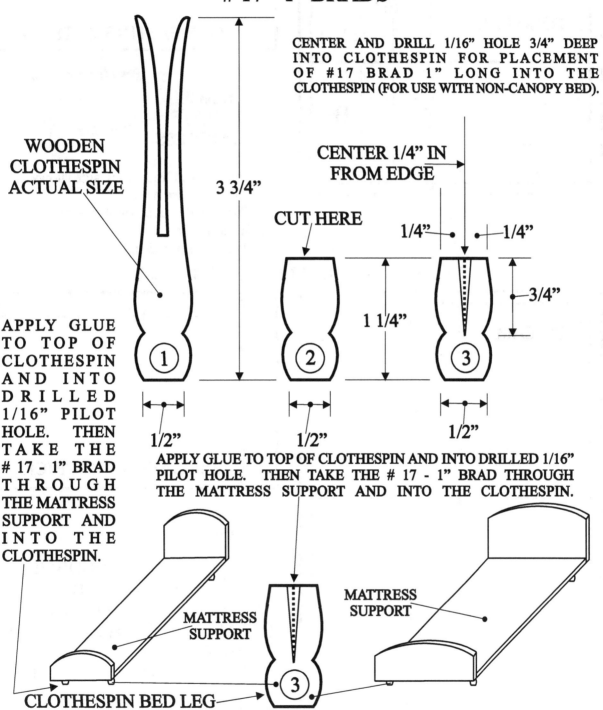

CENTER AND DRILL 1/16" HOLE 3/4" DEEP INTO CLOTHESPIN FOR PLACEMENT OF #17 BRAD 1" LONG INTO THE CLOTHESPIN (FOR USE WITH NON-CANOPY BED).

WOODEN CLOTHESPIN ACTUAL SIZE

CENTER 1/4" IN FROM EDGE

3 3/4"

CUT HERE

1/4"   1/4"

3/4"

1 1/4"

① ② ③

APPLY GLUE TO TOP OF CLOTHESPIN AND INTO DRILLED 1/16" PILOT HOLE. THEN TAKE THE # 17 - 1" BRAD THROUGH THE MATTRESS SUPPORT AND INTO THE CLOTHESPIN.

1/2"   1/2"   1/2"

APPLY GLUE TO TOP OF CLOTHESPIN AND INTO DRILLED 1/16" PILOT HOLE. THEN TAKE THE # 17 - 1" BRAD THROUGH THE MATTRESS SUPPORT AND INTO THE CLOTHESPIN.

MATTRESS SUPPORT

MATTRESS SUPPORT

③

CLOTHESPIN BED LEG

35

FURNITURE: SINGLE BED MATTRESS

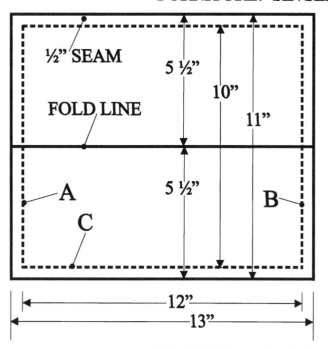

½" SEAM

5 ½"

10"

FOLD LINE

11"

A

5 ½"

B

C

12"

13"

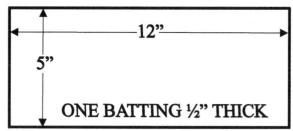

12"

5"

ONE BATTING ½" THICK

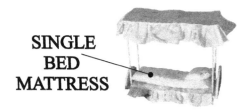

SINGLE
BED
MATTRESS

1. Fold on fold line wrong side shows.
2. Sew ½" seam A and C.
3. Turn inside out so right side shows.
4. Insert batting.
5. Turn ½" seam B in and sew.

FURNITURE: DOUBLE BED MATTRESS

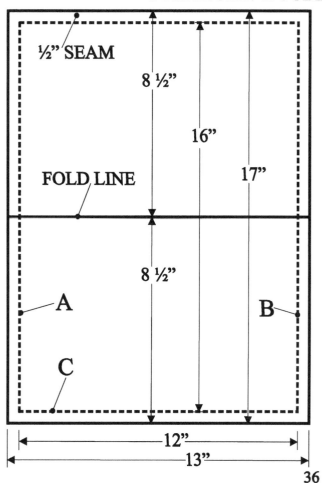

½" SEAM

8 ½"

16"

17"

FOLD LINE

A

8 ½"

B

C

12"

13"

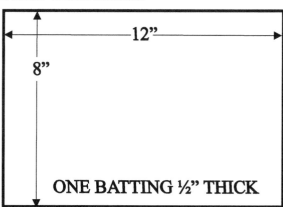

12"

8"

ONE BATTING ½" THICK

DOUBLE
BED
MATTRESS

1. Fold on fold line wrong side shows.
2. Sew ½" seam A and C.
3. Turn inside out so right side shows.
4. Insert batting.
5. Turn ½" seam B in and sew.

SINGLE BED PILLOW

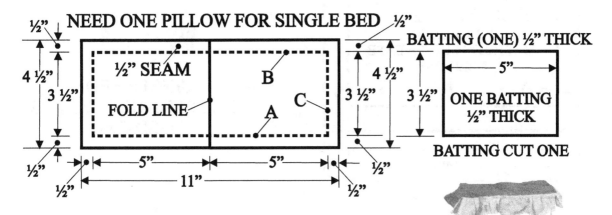

NEED ONE PILLOW FOR SINGLE BED

½"   ½"
4 ½"
3 ½"
½" SEAM   B
FOLD LINE   C
      A
5"   5"
11"
½"   ½"

BATTING (ONE) ½" THICK
4 ½"
3 ½"   3 ½"
5"
ONE BATTING ½" THICK
BATTING CUT ONE
½"
½"

1. Fold on fold line wrong side shows.
2. Sew ½" seam A and C.
3. Turn inside out so right side shows.
4. Insert batting.
5. Turn ½" seam B in and sew.

ONE PILLOW FOR SINGLE BED

DOUBLE BED PILLOW

NEED TWO PILLOWS FOR DOUBLE BED

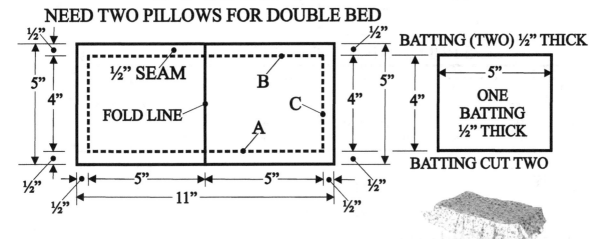

½"   ½"
5"
4"
½" SEAM   B
FOLD LINE   C
      A
5"   5"
11"
½"   ½"

BATTING (TWO) ½" THICK
5"
4"   4"
5"
ONE BATTING ½" THICK
BATTING CUT TWO
½"
½"

1. Fold on fold line wrong side shows.
2. Sew ½" seam A and C.
3. Turn inside out so right side shows.
4. Insert batting.
5. Turn ½" seam B in and sew.

TWO PILLOWS FOR DOUBLE BED

37

FURNITURE: SINGLE AND DOUBLE MATTRESS RUFFLES

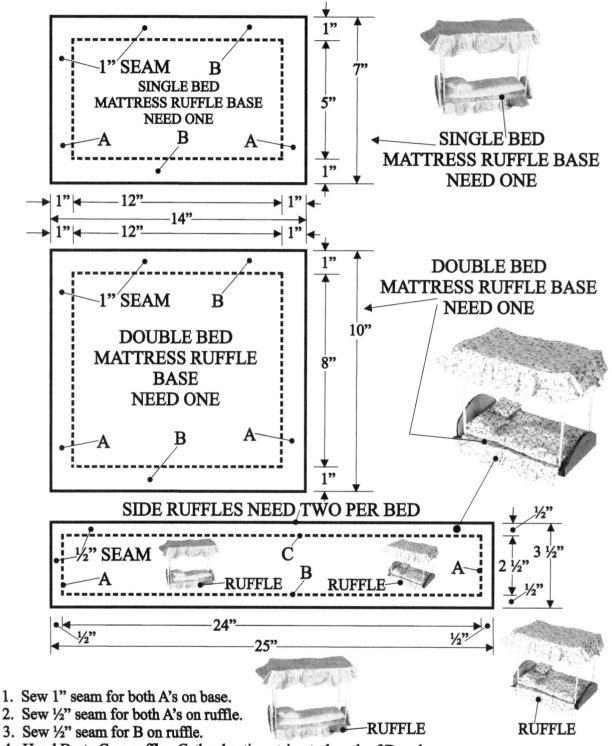

SINGLE BED MATTRESS RUFFLE BASE NEED ONE

1" SEAM   B

SINGLE BED
MATTRESS RUFFLE BASE
NEED ONE

A   B   A

7"   1"   5"   1"

1" | 12" | 1"
14"
1" | 12" | 1"

DOUBLE BED MATTRESS RUFFLE BASE NEED ONE

1" SEAM   B

DOUBLE BED
MATTRESS RUFFLE
BASE
NEED ONE

A   B   A

10"   1"   8"   1"

SIDE RUFFLES NEED TWO PER BED

½" SEAM   C   A
A   RUFFLE   B   RUFFLE

½"   3 ½"   2 ½"   ½"

24"
½"   25"   ½"

RUFFLE   RUFFLE

1. Sew 1" seam for both A's on base.
2. Sew ½" seam for both A's on ruffle.
3. Sew ½" seam for B on ruffle.
4. Hand Baste C on ruffle. Gather basting string to length of B on base.
5. Pin gathered ruffle to base with "right" sides together. Sew 1" seam.
6. Press 1" seam so that it lays toward base. Then sew this down (1/4" from seam already sewn).
7. Top stitch ruffle and base 1/8" seam so ruffle will lay smoothly down side of bed.

38

FURNITURE: SINGLE AND DOUBLE BED CANOPY TOP

SINGLE BED CANOPY TOP

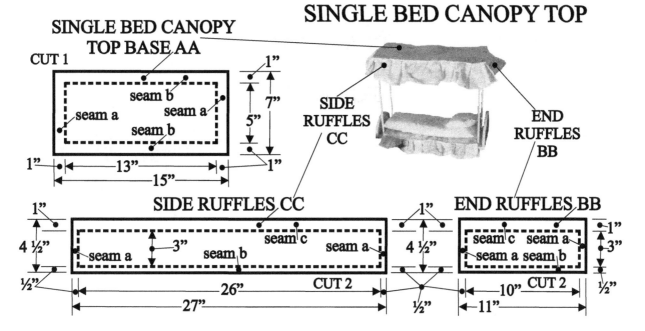

SINGLE BED CANOPY TOP BASE AA

CUT 1

seam b
seam a   seam a
seam b

1"   7"   5"   1"

1"   13"   1"
15"

SIDE RUFFLES CC

END RUFFLES BB

SIDE RUFFLES CC

1"
4 ½"
seam a   3"   seam b   seam c   seam a
½"
26"   CUT 2
27"

END RUFFLES BB

1"
4 ½"
seam c   seam a
seam a   seam b
1"   3"   ½"
10"   CUT 2
½"
11"

1. Sew ½" seam for seam a's on ruffle BB.
2. Sew ½" seam for seam b's on ruffle BB.
3. Hand baste seam c on ruffle BB. Gather basting string to length of b on top canopy base AA.
4. Pin gathered ruffles to top canopy base with "right" sides together. Sew 1" seam.
5. Press 1" seam so that it lays toward base. Then sew this down (1/4" from seam already sewn).
6. Repeat steps 1-5 above using ruffle CC gathering to length of seam a on AA.
7. Top stitch ruffle and base 1/8" seam so ruffle will lay down smoothly on sides of canopy.

DOUBLE BED CANOPY TOP

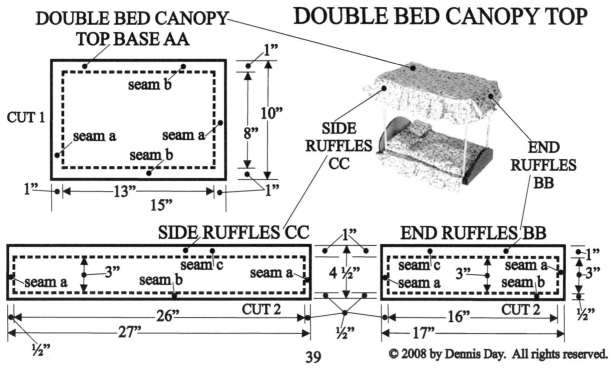

DOUBLE BED CANOPY TOP BASE AA

CUT 1

seam b
seam a   seam a
seam b

1"   10"   8"   1"

1"   13"   1"
15"

SIDE RUFFLES CC

END RUFFLES BB

SIDE RUFFLES CC

seam c
seam a   3"   seam b   seam a
26"   CUT 2
27"
½"

1"
4 ½"
½"

END RUFFLES BB

1"
seam c   seam a
seam a   3"   seam b
1"   3"   ½"
16"   CUT 2
17"

FURNITURE

BLANK PAGE

FOR NOTES

FURNITURE: CRADLE

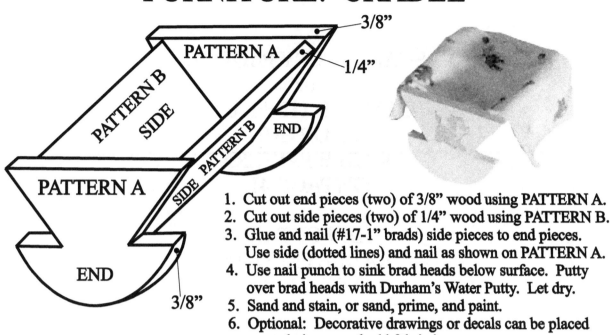

1. Cut out end pieces (two) of 3/8" wood using PATTERN A.
2. Cut out side pieces (two) of 1/4" wood using PATTERN B.
3. Glue and nail (#17-1" brads) side pieces to end pieces.
   Use side (dotted lines) and nail as shown on PATTERN A.
4. Use nail punch to sink brad heads below surface. Putty
   over brad heads with Durham's Water Putty. Let dry.
5. Sand and stain, or sand, prime, and paint.
6. Optional: Decorative drawings or decals can be placed
   on end pieces, and add fabric insert.

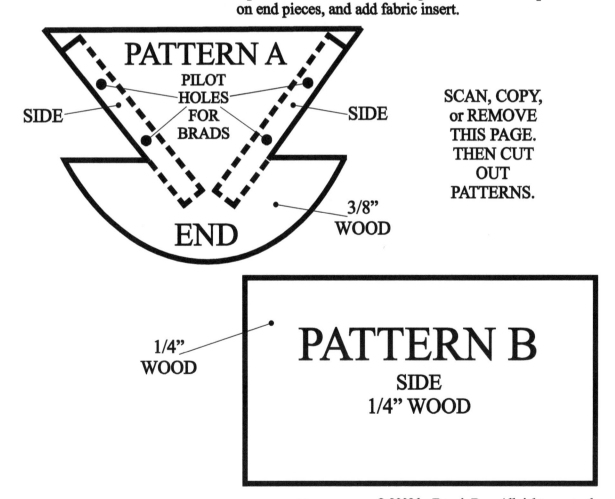

SCAN, COPY,
or REMOVE
THIS PAGE.
THEN CUT
OUT
PATTERNS.

FURNITURE

SCAN or COPY PAGE 41,
or
REMOVE THIS PAGE
TO OBTAIN
CRADLE PATTERNS
ON PAGE 41.

THEN CUT OUT
CRADLE PATTERNS
ON PAGE 41.

INDEX: FURNITURE

Additional book by Dennis Day.

Wooden Dollhouse

You can make a Barbie™ Dollhouse using this plan.

1

Barbie™ Dollhouse Plan Traditional

by Dennis Day

Create a beautiful dollhouse that dreams are made of with this Easy To Build plan. This Do-It-Yourself plan has step-by-step easy to follow instructions. The accompanying drawings and pictures make for easy assembly by the experienced and inexperienced individual. The finished dollhouse will reflect your individual decorating taste. This dollhouse will provide years of enjoyment and be passed on for generations.

Easy To Build
Wooden Dollhouse

Traditional

53" W x 22" D x 52" H • 3 Stories • Eight Rooms

♥ Look for additional Barbie™ Dollhouse Plan Books by Dennis Day at ♥
www.lulu.com/dollhouse

HARDCOPY $19.95 USA

DOWNLOAD $9.95 USA

44

Additional book by Dennis Day.

Wooden Dollhouse

You can make a Barbie™ Dollhouse using this plan.

1 Barbie™ Dollhouse Plan Cottage
by Dennis Day

Create a beautiful dollhouse that dreams are made of with this Easy To Build plan. This Do-It-Yourself plan has step-by-step easy to follow instructions. The accompanying drawings and pictures make for easy assembly by the experienced and inexperienced individual. The finished dollhouse will reflect your individual decorating taste. This dollhouse will provide years of enjoyment and be passed on for generations.

Easy To Build
Wooden Dollhouse

Cottage

33" W x 22" D x 40" H • 2 Stories • Four Rooms

♥ Look for additional Barbie™ Dollhouse Plan Books by Dennis Day at ♥
www.lulu.com/dollhouse

 HARDCOPY $19.95 USA DOWNLOAD $9.95 USA

45

Additional book by Dennis Day.

Wooden Dollhouse

You can make a Barbie™ Dollhouse using this plan.

1

Barbie™ Dollhouse Plan Southern Mansion

by Dennis Day

Create a beautiful dollhouse that dreams are made of with this Easy To Build plan. This Do-It-Yourself plan has step-by-step easy to follow instructions. The accompanying drawings and pictures make for easy assembly by the experienced and inexperienced individual. The finished dollhouse will reflect your individual decorating taste. This dollhouse will provide years of enjoyment and be passed on for generations.

Easy To Build
Wooden Dollhouse

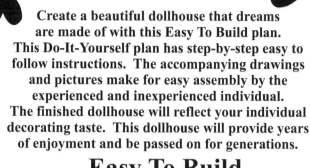

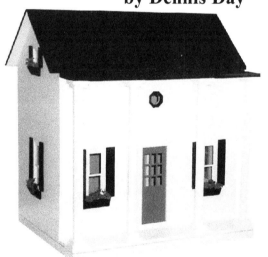

Southern Mansion

33" W x 24" D x 40" H • 2 Stories • Four Rooms

Additional book by Dennis Day.

Wooden Dollhouse

You can make a Barbie™ Dollhouse using this plan.

1 Barbie™ Dollhouse Plan Royal
by Dennis Day

Create a beautiful dollhouse that dreams are made of with this Easy To Build plan. This Do-It-Yourself plan has step-by-step easy to follow instructions. The accompanying drawings and pictures make for easy assembly by the experienced and inexperienced individual. The finished dollhouse will reflect your individual decorating taste. This dollhouse will provide years of enjoyment and be passed on for generations.

Easy To Build

Wooden Dollhouse

Royal

51" W x 21" D x 59" H
• 3 Stories • Seven Rooms

♥ Look for additional Barbie™ Dollhouse Plan Books by Dennis Day at ♥
www.lulu.com/dollhouse

HARDCOPY $19.95 USA

DOWNLOAD $9.95 USA

47

Additional book by Dennis Day.

Wooden Dollhouse

You can make a Barbie™ Dollhouse using this plan.

1 **Barbie™ Dollhouse Plan Ranch**

by Dennis Day

Create a beautiful dollhouse that dreams are made of with this Easy To Build plan. This Do-It-Yourself plan has step-by-step easy to follow instructions. The accompanying drawings and pictures make for easy assembly by the experienced and inexperienced individual. The finished dollhouse will reflect your individual decorating taste. This dollhouse will provide years of enjoyment and be passed on for generations.

Easy To Build
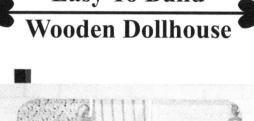
Wooden Dollhouse

Ranch

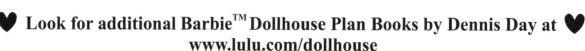

51" W x 21" D x 42" H • 2 Stories • Five Rooms

♥ Look for additional Barbie™ Dollhouse Plan Books by Dennis Day at ♥
www.lulu.com/dollhouse

HARDCOPY $19.95 USA

DOWNLOAD $9.95 USA

48

Additional book by Dennis Day.

Wooden Dollhouse

You can make a Barbie™ Dollhouse using this plan.

1 Barbie™ Dollhouse Plan Southern Colonial
by Dennis Day

Create a beautiful dollhouse that dreams are made of with this Easy To Build plan. This Do-It-Yourself plan has step-by-step easy to follow instructions. The accompanying drawings and pictures make for easy assembly by the experienced and inexperienced individual. The finished dollhouse will reflect your individual decorating taste. This dollhouse will provide years of enjoyment and be passed on for generations.

Easy To Build
Wooden Dollhouse

Southern Colonial

51" W x 30" D x 43" H
• 2 Stories • Four Rooms

 HARDCOPY $19.95 USA DOWNLOAD $9.95 USA

Additional book by Dennis Day.

Wooden Dollhouse

You can make a Barbie™ Dollhouse using this plan.

1

Barbie™ Dollhouse Plan Log Manor

by Dennis Day

Create a beautiful dollhouse that dreams are made of with this Easy To Build plan. This Do-It-Yourself plan has step-by-step easy to follow instructions. The accompanying drawings and pictures make for easy assembly by the experienced and inexperienced individual. The finished dollhouse will reflect your individual decorating taste. This dollhouse will provide years of enjoyment and be passed on for generations.

Easy To Build
Wooden Dollhouse

Log Manor

55" W x 21" D x 59" H • 3 Stories • Seven Rooms

Look for additional Barbie™ Dollhouse Plan Books by Dennis Day at
www.lulu.com/dollhouse

 HARDCOPY $19.95 USA DOWNLOAD $9.95 USA

Additional book by Dennis Day.

Wooden Dollhouse

You can make a Barbie™ Dollhouse using this plan.

1

Barbie™ Dollhouse Plan
Log Home
by Dennis Day

Create a beautiful dollhouse that dreams are made of with this Easy To Build plan. This Do-It-Yourself plan has step-by-step easy to follow instructions. The accompanying drawings and pictures make for easy assembly by the experienced and inexperienced individual. The finished dollhouse will reflect your individual decorating taste. This dollhouse will provide years of enjoyment and be passed on for generations.

Easy To Build
Wooden Dollhouse

Log Home

55" W x 22" D x 42" H   • 2 Stories • Four Rooms

♥ Look for additional Barbie™ Dollhouse Plan Books by Dennis Day at ♥
www.lulu.com/dollhouse

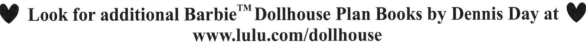

HARDCOPY $19.95 USA

DOWNLOAD $9.95 USA

51

Additional book by Dennis Day.

Wooden Dollhouse

You can make a Barbie™ Dollhouse using this plan.

1 Barbie™ Dollhouse Plan Log Cabin
by Dennis Day

Create a beautiful dollhouse that dreams are made of with this Easy To Build plan. This Do-It-Yourself plan has step-by-step easy to follow instructions. The accompanying drawings and pictures make for easy assembly by the experienced and inexperienced individual. The finished dollhouse will reflect your individual decorating taste. This dollhouse will provide years of enjoyment and be passed on for generations.

Easy To Build
Wooden Dollhouse

Log Cabin

46" W x 22" D x 42" H • 2 Stories • Four Rooms

Additional book by Dennis Day.

Wooden Dollhouses

You can make one, two, or three Barbie™ Dollhouses with furniture using these plans.

4 Barbie™ Dollhouse Plans Book One

by Dennis Day

Create three beautiful dollhouses with furniture that dreams are made of with these Easy To Build plans. These Do-It-Yourself plans have step-by-step easy to follow instructions. The accompanying drawings and pictures make for easy assembly by the experienced and inexperienced individual. The finished dollhouses and furniture will reflect your individual decorating taste. These dollhouses and furniture will provide years of enjoyment and be passed on for generations.

Easy To Build

Wooden Dollhouses

Traditional
- 3 Stories • Eight Rooms
53" W x 22" D x 52" H

Southern Mansion
- 2 Stories • Four Rooms
33" W x 24" D x 40" H

Cottage
- 2 Stories • Four Rooms
33" W x 22" D x 40" H

Furniture
- Living Room • Bedrooms
- Kitchen • All Rooms

♥ **Look for additional Barbie™ Dollhouse Plan Books by Dennis Day at** ♥
www.lulu.com/dollhouse

 HARDCOPY $39.95 USA  **DOWNLOAD $19.95 USA**

53

Additional book by Dennis Day.

Wooden Dollhouses

You can make one, two, or three Barbie™ Dollhouses with furniture using these plans.

4 Barbie™ Dollhouse Plans Book Two
by Dennis Day

Create three beautiful dollhouses with furniture that dreams are made of with these Easy To Build plans. These Do-It-Yourself plans have step-by-step easy to follow instructions. The accompanying drawings and pictures make for easy assembly by the experienced and inexperienced individual. The finished dollhouses and furniture will reflect your individual decorating taste. These dollhouses and furniture will provide years of enjoyment and be passed on for generations.

Easy To Build
Wooden Dollhouses

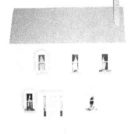

Royal
- 3 Stories • Seven Rooms
51" W x 21" D x 59" H

Southern Colonial
- 2 Stories • Four Rooms
51" W x 30" D x 43" H

Ranch
- 2 Stories • Five Rooms
51" W x 21" D x 42" H

Furniture
- Living Room • Bedrooms
- Kitchen • All Rooms

♥ Look for additional Barbie™ Dollhouse Plan Books by Dennis Day at ♥
www.lulu.com/dollhouse

HARDCOPY $39.95 USA

DOWNLOAD $19.95 USA

54

Additional book by Dennis Day.

Wooden Dollhouses

You can make one, two, or three Barbie™ Dollhouses with furniture using these plans.

4 Barbie™ Dollhouse Plans Book Three
by Dennis Day

Create three beautiful dollhouses with furniture that dreams are made of with these Easy To Build plans. These Do-It-Yourself plans have step-by-step easy to follow instructions. The accompanying drawings and pictures make for easy assembly by the experienced and inexperienced individual. The finished dollhouses and furniture will reflect your individual decorating taste. These dollhouses and furniture will provide years of enjoyment and be passed on for generations.

Easy To Build
Wooden Dollhouses

Log Manor
• 3 Stories • Seven Rooms
55" W x 21" D x 59" H

Log Home
• 2 Stories • Four Rooms
55" W x 22" D x 42" H

Log Cabin
• 2 Stories • Four Rooms
46" W x 22" D x 42" H

Furniture
• Living Room • Bedrooms
• Kitchen • All Rooms

♥ **Look for additional Barbie™ Dollhouse Plan Books by Dennis Day at** ♥
www.lulu.com/dollhouse

HARDCOPY $39.95 USA

DOWNLOAD $19.95 USA

55

       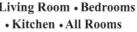

56

Additional book by Dennis Day.

Wooden Dollhouses

You can make one, two, or three Barbie™ Dollhouses with furniture using these plans.

4 Barbie™ Dollhouse Plans Book Five

by Dennis Day

Create three beautiful dollhouses with furniture that dreams are made of with these Easy To Build plans. These Do-It-Yourself plans have step-by-step easy to follow instructions. The accompanying drawings and pictures make for easy assembly by the experienced and inexperienced individual. The finished dollhouses and furniture will reflect your individual decorating taste. These dollhouses and furniture will provide years of enjoyment and be passed on for generations.

Easy To Build Wooden Dollhouses

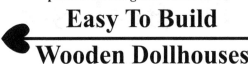

Southern Colonial
- 2 Stories • Four Rooms
51" W x 30" D x 43" H

Ranch
- 2 Stories • Five Rooms
51" W x 21" D x 42" H

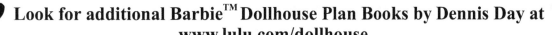

Log Home
- 2 Stories • Four Rooms
55" W x 22" D x 42" H

Furniture
- Living Room • Bedrooms
- Kitchen • All Rooms

♥ **Look for additional Barbie™ Dollhouse Plan Books by Dennis Day at** ♥
www.lulu.com/dollhouse

HARDCOPY $39.95 USA

DOWNLOAD $19.95 USA

57

Additional book by Dennis Day.

Wooden Dollhouses

You can make one, two, or three Barbie™ Dollhouses with furniture using these plans.

4 Barbie™ Dollhouse Plans Book Six

by Dennis Day

Create three beautiful dollhouses with furniture that dreams are made of with these Easy To Build plans. These Do-It-Yourself plans have step-by-step easy to follow instructions. The accompanying drawings and pictures make for easy assembly by the experienced and inexperienced individual. The finished dollhouses and furniture will reflect your individual decorating taste. These dollhouses and furniture will provide years of enjoyment and be passed on for generations.

Easy To Build

Wooden Dollhouses

Log Cabin

- 2 Stories • Four Rooms
46" W x 22" D x 42" H

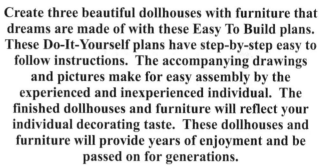

Southern Mansion

- 2 Stories • Four Rooms
33" W x 24" D x 40" H

Cottage

- 2 Stories • Four Rooms
33" W x 22" D x 40" H

Furniture

- Living Room • Bedrooms
- Kitchen • All Rooms

♥ **Look for additional Barbie™ Dollhouse Plan Books by Dennis Day at** ♥
www.lulu.com/dollhouse

 HARDCOPY $39.95 USA

DOWNLOAD $19.95 USA

58

CPSIA information can be obtained
at www.ICGtesting.com
Printed in the USA
LVHW060025140320
650070LV00016B/187